Single Not Sad

Ditching
the stereotype
that all single women
are broken, bitter,
or bored

COMPILED BY

Kimmoly LaBoo

For information regarding special discounts for bulk purchases contact the Publisher:

LaBoo Publishing Enterprise, LLC

staff@laboopublishing.com
www.laboopublishing.com

All information is solely considered as the point of view of the authors.

Love yourself first,
because that's who
you'll spend the rest
of your life with.

~ UNKNOWN

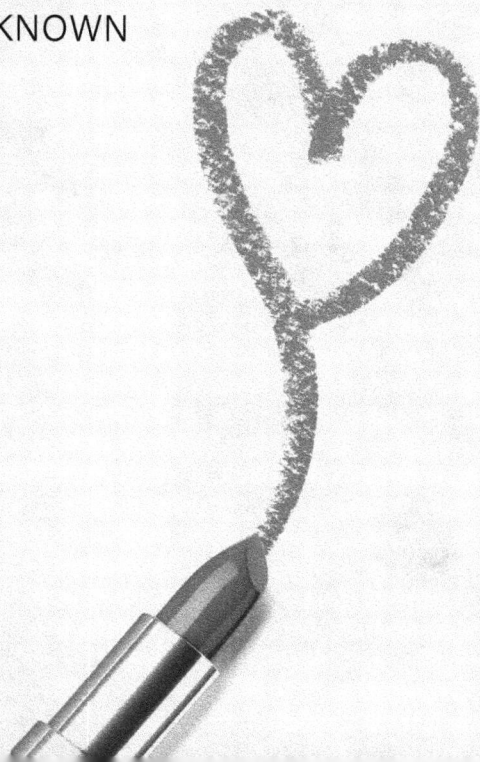

Contents

Introduction 1

Unashamed. Unbothered. Unmarried. Unstoppable.
    Tamlyn Johnson. 3

You Are Somebody
    Tammie Thacker 27

And the Clock Strikes Twelve
    Alison Assanah-Carroll 35

Three Strikes
    LaRay Williams 53

Choosing Joy: A Journey Through Singleness, Faith, and Self-Love
    Carrie Haley 59

The Upside of Divorce: This Is What Power Looks Like
    Mary Murrill. 69

Alone at Last
    Kimmoly LaBoo. 77

50 Things Happily Single Women Do With Their Time. 83

Introduction

There's a narrative the world loves to tell—that single women are somehow unfinished. That we're bitter, bored, broken, or just biding our time until someone shows up to "complete" us.

But here's the truth: we are not waiting to become whole. We already are.

According to the U.S. Census Bureau, nearly **one in three women over the age of 40 in the U.S. is single**—yet society still treats singleness like a problem to be solved instead of a life to be celebrated.

This book is a declaration, a celebration, and a reminder. *Single Not Sad* was born out of a desire to shatter outdated myths about singleness and replace them with truth—God's truth. Being single is not a punishment, a problem to fix, or a season to simply endure. It is a sacred time, filled with purpose, joy, and growth.

Think of this season like a garden—rich with potential, beauty, and bloom. It may not look like everyone else's, but it's flourishing in its own divine timing.

If you've ever felt like your life is on pause because of your relationship status, let this be your permission to press play. Psalm 16:11 says, "In Your presence is fullness of joy." That joy is available to you right now. Not when you get married. Not when you're chosen by someone else. But now—because you've already been chosen by God.

In these pages, you'll find encouragement, truth, and real stories from women who are living full, vibrant lives—single and satisfied. You'll be reminded that your identity is rooted in who God says you are, not in your relationship status.

So let's ditch the myth and rewrite the story. Let's live this season fully, joyfully, and unapologetically.

Welcome to *Single Not Sad*.

Unashamed. Unbothered. Unmarried. Unstoppable.

TAMLYN JOHNSON

The moment I sat on the sofa in my therapist's office, he took one look at me and later told me the one word that he wrote:

Pitiful.

We laugh about it now, but back then, nothing was funny. He said I looked like a frightened kitten—backed into a corner, trapped with no way out. And he wasn't lying.

I was grieving the kind of losses that make a person want to raise the white flag—my security, my marriage, my home, my stability, my identity.

Gone.

Everything was gone in a few short minutes.

It has been sixty-nine days since I last laid eyes on my husband. I hadn't planned on leaving him. I didn't map it out. I didn't pack intentionally or have moving trucks reserved for a specific date. I wasn't prepared for the unraveling that was about to happen. I wasn't ready for the shift.

It started on a gray Friday morning in May—the kind of morning that feels heavy before it even begins. I'd thrown on some sweats, planning to pick up my grandkids, when I got the call. My husband had been arrested at a nearby gas station for traffic violations and taken to an unknown location.

Minutes later, as I lifted my head after lacing up my sneakers, I glanced out our bedroom window and saw a sea of officers walking toward our home, down the driveway. Somehow, they opened the garage and entered.

One female officer, flanked by an assembly of male officers who said little, barked orders. One of them—an angel in disguise—quietly whispered to me, "Don't panic, Mrs. Franklin. Just grab what you can—your purse, important documents, birth certificates, social security cards, and license. Everything will be okay."

But it didn't feel okay.

The moment felt surreal.

"You have fifteen minutes," said the officer, looking down at her watch, "to gather what you can and leave the house—or you'll be arrested for trespassing when the timer goes off."

I called my sister in a panic. She picked up on the first ring and before I could utter a word, she said, "Let me call you right back." In the frantic chaos, I yelled, "I don't have time! I'm being evicted from my home right now!" A short time later, she and my two brothers showed up when I needed them most. Without wavering, she said, "Come stay with me. I've got you and Des." And she meant it. She opened her home to me and my daughter with open arms- no judgment, no questions, just love.

I showed up at her back door with barely anything—no furniture, no memories. Just the house keys that no longer had a home, a plastic trash bag with a few familiar items, the shabby sweats and battered sneakers I was wearing, my crushed spirit, and a life that felt shattered overnight.

I was working a part-time job. No benefits. No stability.

My husband was gone.

My blended family scattered.

An entire mess.

I stood frozen on the porch of our five-bedroom home, watching everything we'd built over seventeen years get hauled away on large flatbed trucks—sofas, tables, plants, clothes, our children's shoes, coats, lamps, kitchen appliances, lawn furniture. Every single possession.

Item by item, the life we created was being tossed around, packed up, and thrown away—right in front of me.

The officers sneered and laughed.

And I stood there—humiliated and helpless—watching my life reduced to piles of broken memories.

That moment?

Rock bottom.

But it was also the beginning.

The Turning Point

What I couldn't see then was that God wasn't punishing me—He was preparing me. He was pruning away everything that couldn't go with me into the next chapter. God is all-wise. Every cut had a purpose. Every loss held meaning. He was clearing space to rebuild me to his original design—strong, free, whole.

But the process?

Painful.

It hurt like hell.

The pain wasn't just emotional—it showed up in my body. What followed in the days, weeks, and months after the eviction was a steady breakdown of everything, even my physical well-being. My hair started falling out in patches. Angry red bumps covered my neck, chest, arms, back, and hands. I was itching and scratching like a drug addict who needed a fix. White patches appeared on my face.

I was having my own "Job (from the Bible) experience."

My body was breaking down under the weight of everything I had carried for so long.

And the nightmare didn't stop there.

I was rear-ended by a new driver while waiting at a traffic light. Sideswiped—my car severely damaged—while backing out of a parking space. And one day, I missed a step and tumbled down a full flight of hardwood stairs—bruised, battered, black and blue, and shaken to my core.

It was as if my body was crying out the pain my mouth couldn't speak.

But through all of that, something deeper was happening.

I wasn't just losing a marriage—I was peeling away the version of myself that was never meant to be.

The door behind me didn't slam. It closed with the finality of a casket.

Still. Silent. Gone.

At that moment, I realized—

I was no longer a wife.

No longer a resident.

No longer . . . home.

But I was still prayerful and holding on to hope with all my might.

That Friday night, I sat on the side of the twin bed, looking at my phone, waiting for a call. I truly believed we'd work it out. Everything would be okay. I thought he'd call me to come pick him up any minute—and just like times past, we'd talk, I'd cry, he'd promise to fix it, and we'd keep moving forward.

I thought love meant staying, no matter what.

I thought commitment meant compromising—even if it hurt me or cost me myself.

I was a ride-or-die wife.

But his arrest?

It was a holy disruption.

Divine intervention.

If he had come home that same day—or the next, or even the Monday after—I would've stayed. I would've gone right back with him, put on the wife face, and convinced myself we'd be okay, even if we had to sleep under a bridge.

I wasn't planning to leave that morning. I just wanted to pick up my grandkids and be Gram.

But God had other plans.

And sometimes grace doesn't look like soft whispers and gentle nudges.

Sometimes it looks like helicopters, sirens, flatbed trucks, and a garage full of officers telling you to go.

And now, years later, I can finally say, "Thank God he didn't come back that weekend. Thank God for granting me sixty-nine days."

Because if he had, I'd still be there—still shrinking, still sacrificing, still surviving.

But I'm not there anymore.

I'm here.

And there are new beginnings here.

Reclaiming Me

I gave up my name without hesitation.

No hyphen. No uncertainty. No second thoughts.

I can laugh about it now—because I finally understand what he meant when he called me "pitiful."

My identity had been stripped, and giving up my maiden name was the beginning of that.

I didn't delay for a second. I was thrilled to take my husband's last name—just like every woman in my family had before me. I had watched my mother, my sisters, my grandmother, and even my great-grandmother quietly surrender their maiden names without flinching. It was tradition. It was expected. It was simply what the women in my family did.

But I never knew that my identity wasn't just something on paper—it was both literal and symbolic. Retrieving my maiden name after the divorce wasn't easy. I had to jump through hoops, making in-person visits to the Social Security office, banks, and the courthouse during post-COVID-19 restricted hours—it was a whole process to undo what had been done.

Then I had to relearn myself and get to know who I really was. I had to learn that I love comedy and laughing until my stomach aches. I had to rediscover that I'm happiest when I'm traveling and dining in swanky restaurants all over the world. I had to embrace all my OCD quirks and accept that they're okay. That *I'm* okay.

And I didn't need to feel bad about who God made me to be—
my fearfully and wonderfully made self.

I laid everything on the altar of what I thought marriage should
be—myself, my dreams, my voice, my boundaries. I believed love
was about sacrifice. I watched my parents and carried the indel-
ible imprints that supported my position. I thought that if I gave
it all, I'd get it all. I thought my marriage would be different from
what I witnessed growing up. I genuinely thought it would be the
fix—the panacea, the covering for every wound we both carried.

Sure, we had disagreements before the wedding. But I chalked it
up to stress, to passion, to growing pains—because you couldn't
tell me it wasn't love. I believed that once we said, "I do," everything
would magically smooth itself out. The ring would transform
dysfunction into stability—and most importantly, loyalty.

I believed in happily ever after. Heck, I believed in Santa Claus
until I was a pre-teen. I believed in the fairytale of marriage. I
expected a love that healed, validated, and celebrated me, daily.
I thought our new life together would wash away the red flags,
the chaos, the doubt. I believed our union would dissolve any
pain—and that love was all we needed.

Love would be enough.

But love without accountability is like building a house on sand.
The foundation won't hold.

And ignoring red flags is foolish. It doesn't make them disappear. It just makes the consequences hurt more.

I saw the signals—clear as day. I heard the deafening warnings—loud as a bullhorn. When we were dating, he was still emotionally entangled in a turbulent marriage that hadn't yet come to a legal end.

But what did I do?

Put my head in the sand.

Yup.

I quenched the Holy Spirit, silenced my intuition, and told myself it didn't matter.

I was certain that once we got married, everything would somehow reset. You know, a fresh start. Like the Word says, love conquers all. And that love could override reality.

But it didn't.

Because the truth is, being separated still means being married—no matter how many years have passed. And if someone is still legally bound to another, no matter what story they tell, they are not fully available. Healing after a breakup takes time.

You can't end one chapter and expect to step into the next one whole. Real healing needs space. It needs time to grieve, to ponder, to grow. Without it, you're just carrying old wounds into fresh places. Trying to pour new wine into old wineskins.

Admittedly, I was green. Gullible. Easily manipulated by charm, by hope, and by my own desire for a happy ending.

"Oh, I say, and I say it again—I was had! I was took! I was hood-winked! Bamboozled! Led astray! Run amok!" And by my own naivety.

But here's what I know now:

I may have lost my name back then, but I've reclaimed so much more.

I am single, not sad. Better not bitter. Whole, not broken.

And I am mindful—never again will I exchange my identity for the fantasy of love.

Rising from Rock Bottom

Low self-esteem had trickled into every part of my life. Relationships. Work. Finances. My self-image.

I was like the best supporting actress in my life's performance. I was pleasing everyone—except me.

I was surviving. I wasn't living.

Day sixty-nine was the turning point. It was like the lights flipped on, and I woke up from a seventeen-year fog. I realized . . .

My God! I'm homeless.

I was a wife. A mother. A woman with multiple degrees. A grandmother. A daughter. And yet—I had no place to call home.

Something about this just didn't add up.

But that day, I stopped being a victim and started being a survivor.

The Lies I Believed

I used to think love meant staying—even when it hurt.

That commitment meant compromise—even it cost me myself.

That being married meant being whole.

But marriage didn't fix my wounds—it magnified them.

I traded my last name for a title.

My voice for the illusion of inclusion.

My whole self . . . for someone else's validation.

Even after the ring was placed on my finger, I still felt incomplete.

Because marriage doesn't erase insecurity—it amplifies it.

Waking Up

Somewhere between braiding hair, throwing a load in the washing machine, and preparing stuffed shells for dinner, I disappeared.

I was so consumed with being his wife, their mother, and everyone's peacekeeper—that I forgot me.

I was a woman first.

Our home was never still. There were people in every room. Voices in every corner. Laughter. Yelling. TVs competing with each other—*SportsCenter* always singing, "da-na-na, da-na-na" and a video game going on in another room. The sound of chaos became the soundtrack of my life.

But somewhere under all that noise . . . I lost the sound of me. There was no B side. No "me" side. I silenced myself so often that I forgot how I sounded.

I didn't just forget who I was—I stopped asking.

The silence? The loss?

It taught me to listen. To feel. To find my way back—to me, to the woman I was designed to be, not the role.

When the cops entered our home, my journey to singlehood began. Now, don't get me wrong—I left the house by force because they had guns. But leaving the marriage? **That was a choice.**

For more than two months, I lived apart from my husband. And in that quiet space, something deep within me began to stir. After nearly twenty years of moving through the fog of denial, dysfunction, and distraction, I started to hear my voice again.

The long healing hikes and trail walks . . .

The early morning and late-night chats with my sister . . .

The weekly sessions with my therapist . . .

All of it helped guide me back to myself.

No blaring TV.

No raised voices.

No one demanding.

Just me, stillness, and the whispers of the Holy Spirit.

I hadn't realized how controlled I'd become until a friend said, "Girl, you were under total control." I didn't realize how quiet my voice had grown until I sat alone in the stillness.

It was like tuning in to a radio station that had always been there—but the static had finally cleared. The Holy Spirit started speaking louder. Guiding me. Healing me. I was finally tuning in.

One morning, with no grand plan and barely any resources, I woke up and heard it clearly: *"Go to the courthouse today, and file for divorce."*

And then: *"I will take care of you. Just go."*

I had no money. No plan. And many questions.

But I went.

I moved.

And God was with me every step of the way.

I'm Free

I once thought being single meant being incomplete.

But the truth?

No one can complete you.

Not a ring. Not a title. And not a man.

Wholeness doesn't come from being chosen by someone else. It comes from choosing yourself.

And it would take years—and unimaginable losses—for me to finally understand that.

I didn't just want to be loved. I wanted to be validated. I wanted the ring, the title, the role.

But what I didn't understand back then was that the vows wouldn't quiet my insecurities. Instead, they amplified them.

Feeling inadequate and dealing with low self-esteem? That's putting it lightly. I felt downright ashamed that I had made it into adulthood unmarried. It was like carrying an invisible weight in every room, especially around family.

And the saddest part? Even after I said, "I do," that shame did not go away. It deepened.

What the heck?

Marriage didn't make me feel more whole. It made me feel more dependent. I became a stay-at-home mom, a damsel in distress—always looking for my husband to rescue me from fear, from self-doubt, from myself. I felt needy, like I couldn't make it without him.

But that wasn't love. That was **bondage.**

And now I know—it was a trick of the enemy. What seemed like tradition was really a quiet struggle within. A lie that told me that I was not enough unless I was married.

I've learned that I don't need to be attached to be loved.

I don't have to do or fix everything myself.

I don't have to exchange my peace for anyone's presence.

Yes, I miss cuddling sometimes. But I love the sound of stillness and the coolness of the entire bed.

I love knowing in my soul that I am enough.

I have **always** been enough.

Strong, Soft Girl Era

And now?

Now, I'm living in my Soft Girl Era.

When I was married, my husband was my protector, and I was a self-proclaimed handywoman—DIY project queen, thank you very much. I took pride in being resourceful, in rolling up my sleeves and getting things done. I always had a project going. I painted entire rooms, converted our garage into a classroom for my mentees, patched holes in walls—like the time one of our kids launched a cue ball straight through the basement sheetrock. I hung shelves, measured and leveled frames, drilled curtain rods into drywall, and even mowed the lawn when needed.

I did all of that because I thought I was being helpful—trying to hold everything together while it was all falling apart.

But this season?

This season is different.

This is the season that I choose softness. I choose peace. I choose ease. I choose rest.

There was a time I wore the title of wife like a badge of honor, like a flashback to my Girl Scout days. *Look at me, my sash full of pins, turning this house into a home!* And at the time, it felt empowering.

But now?

Get someone else to do it.

Seriously.

I've retired the handywoman hat and toolbelt. In fact, I haven't seen either since I moved out of my sister's house and into my own place. Instead, I have a wonderful team of professional handymen on speed dial. If something breaks, they fix it. If I buy a large picture or heavy mirror, they hang it. If anything squeaks, chirps, drips, or needs assembling, they handle it, not me. I'm done lifting anything except my finger—to make a call.

I don't need validation. I have nothing to prove. I've been through enough to know that I am fully capable. But I don't have to do it all.

This Soft Girl Era isn't about being helpless or powerless. It's about choices. It's about choosing me. It's about being whole.

I'm embracing the version of me that no longer feels the need to handle everything alone.

And if we're being honest . . .

You can lie next to someone every night and still feel alone. You can be married and still feel invisible, untouched, unheard.

I know—because I've lived it.

Don't get me wrong. Intimacy is beautiful. I loved cuddling. I cherished those moments.

But let me tell you something—the way these hot flashes are set up right now? I now cherish sprawling across my king-sized bed, ceiling fan spinning on high, and the thermostat locked at a cool sixty-nine degrees—year-round.

Don't judge. That's peace, too.

Did I mention how much I enjoy the feel of cool bamboo sheets on my skin, without someone else's body heat making me sweat like I just hiked Diamond Head?

Here's the truth no one tells you:

You can have sex and still feel disconnected.

You can share a bed and still feel untouched.

You can be married and still feel like you're living alone.

My marriage was dynamic—not all bad, not all good. Just . . . dynamic.

But when that kind of relationship turns into a constant cycle of feeling unseen, unloved, and like you're just pretending? That's when you start to lose who you are.

But now, I've found myself. I've made peace with who I am. And I enjoy my company.

I've learned how to meet my emotional needs without begging or waiting for permission from anyone else to do so.

So now?

I'm not just surviving—I'm thriving. I'm no longer burdened by who I used to be or who I thought I needed to be. I'm not performing. I'm not seeking approval. I'm not shrinking or dimming my light. I'm living authentically.

I am unashamed—free from guilt, fear, or worrying what anyone thinks. I carry parts of my past not as baggage but as a badge. Every scar, every wound, every choice—it's part of my story. And I refuse to be ashamed of any of it.

If *unbothered* was a person?

I am her.

I'm no longer stirred by the opinions or expectations of others. Now I say—with peace, pride, and joy—*it is what it is, and it was what it was.*

I am unmarried, not undone. Not a puzzle missing a piece. Not missing my right arm. Not a story missing a plot. I am whole. I am complete.

If *unstoppable* were a person?

I am her.

Because every time life throws a knockout blow, I get back up. I've known rock-bottom. I've lost loved ones. I lost my firstborn son and both my parents. I watched my home, my family, my marriage, and my sense of stability disappear like vapor.

And still—I rose.

Almost ten years ago, long before my life unraveled, I wrote a book called *How to Become an Unstoppable Black Woman.*

At the time, I was speaking it by faith. I had no idea that I was writing for me.

Because now?

I am her.

Every word in that book was preparing me for this moment.

Now, I don't just speak those words—I *live* them.

Now, I'm unfolding in power.

Every day reveals another layer of who I really am. Every moment is a chance to write a new chapter—not as someone's wife, but as *me*.

This version of me is soft, yes.

But she's strong.

She laughs easily.

She sleeps peacefully.

Thinks clearly.

Loves deeply.

She listens when God speaks and obeys when the Holy Spirit whispers.

And she walks boldly into her future.

I am not just single.

I am free.

I am whole.

I am complete.

And here I stand—

Unashamed. Unbothered. Unmarried. Unstoppable. Unfolding
in power.

You Are Somebody

TAMMIE THACKER

I believe my life was doomed even before I entered this world on March 19 in the mid-1960s. My birth mother made the conscious decision to put me up for adoption right after giving birth. I don't know why, and one day, I hope I'll have the chance to ask her.

I don't remember how many foster homes I was placed in during my early years, but I do recall one in particular. I was four years old. I remember a big, beautiful house with a lot of rooms. I thought I would finally have my own room with my own bed. I was sadly mistaken.

That house is where I experienced physical, emotional, and sexual abuse. I remember the tall man who did things to me and then made me sleep in the dark, damp, dirty basement. I wasn't given a blanket to sleep on. I just sat in that smelly place and quietly cried myself to sleep. The cruelty I experienced there, before being moved to a new home, shaped my emotional makeup.

When I turned five, I was adopted by a Christian family. My new father was a bishop, and my new mother was a mission-ary. I thought I was finally safe—that I wouldn't have to endure any more cruel treatment. I have mixed feelings about what I experienced at that home. I never had a great relationship with my adoptive mother, and I never felt motherly love. My basic needs were met, but something was missing. I never felt com-fortable, and I was often beaten because of my attitude and my mouth.

In my early teens, I was again the victim of repeated sex-ual abuse. When I finally felt brave enough to tell my mother what was happening, her response stunned me. She called me a Jezebel and a nasty, fast-tail girl. I was devasted! The terms she used to describe me, I didn't even understand what those words meant. And if that wasn't bad enough, I received one of the worst beatings of my life—because of who I had accused. I couldn't understand it. I had thought she would hold me and tell me everything would be okay. But that didn't happen.

I became depressed. I felt rejected, unloved, bitter, angry, and alone. From that day on, I knew I was on my own. I had no one else.

As I got older and tried to process the abuse, I became angrier. The bitterness really began to settle in. I suffered silently and kept to myself. After high school, I moved into a rooming house and started using drugs, drinking, and selling my body to pay rent and put food on the table. I thought doing all that would take away the emotional turmoil and pain I was feeling.

Even though I had been raised in the church from the age of five, I couldn't understand why God wasn't helping me. I questioned Him on several occasions. I don't remember praying, because I really didn't have that kind of relationship with him.

One night after being taken advantage of, I thought about ending it all. I felt that no one loved me anyway, so who would even miss me? I had the bottle of Tylenol in my hand, and I poured out all fifty pills and put them in my mouth. But then I heard a voice say, *If you kill yourself, you'll go to hell.* I immediately spit the pills out of my mouth.

I started crying and asked God to forgive me. It was at this point that I realized I needed to find a Church to get my soul right.

Soon after, a college friend invited me to a musical concert at Macedonia Baptist Church in Mount Vernon, New York, so I went. I listened to the various songs, but one song touched me—*Near the Cross.* I had heard it many times before, but this time it did something to me. I began to cry.

After the concert, my friend talked me into joining the Westchester Mass Choir, a community choir directed by the late Bishop Michel White. I also joined the church two weeks later— and accepted Jesus as my Savior.

That was the beginning of my spiritual journey—and when I began to understand Tammie. I realized that I lacked self-love. In fact, I hated myself. But I began to learn that self-love is a positive state of appreciation and respect for who you are. When you love yourself, it leads to a happier, more fulfilled life.

I had never experienced this before. I had held onto too much hate, anger, depression, rejection, and unforgiveness for too long.

But then I stopped smoking the weed. I stopped drinking hard liquor. And eventually, I even stopped having sex. As I did all this, I began to feel good about myself. I realized that if I truly wanted to move forward in my spiritual walk—I had to love Tammie.

The first commandment is "Love the Lord your God with all your heart and with all your soul and with all your mind and with all your strength." And the second is, "You shall love your neighbor as yourself. There is no other commandment greater than these" (Mark 12:30-31, NKJV).

The first commandment is clear and straightforward—love God first and love Him most. But the second commandment has an expectation built into it—that you must love *yourself*.

That was an eye-opening revelation for me, especially after all those years of self-hatred. I finally understood that self-love was a necessity—it's the foundation on which love for your neighbor is built. Jesus was saying that I must love my neighbor as I love myself.

Right then, I prayed to God and asked Him to forgive me for all my years of self-hate. As I began to grow spiritually and heal emotionally, I learned that self-love is a natural part of who we are. I had been missing it because of my early childhood trauma.

Self-love includes self-care, and self-preservation—and I had failed in those areas. But as I began to let go of the emotional baggage I was holding onto, I realized that loving Tammie—and believing that I had purpose—meant accepting myself with all my flaws, mistakes, faults, and bad decisions. I had to trust the process.

I began to get involved in different areas of the church and began studying the Word of God. I wanted to keep busy. I was determined to become a better person and continue down the road to emotional healing. I stayed away from anything that would mess with my emotions. That was very important to me because I didn't want to fall back into my old patterns.

Honestly, the road that I was walking, wasn't easy. I had to fight daily—against depression, against unforgiveness. I was serving in the ministry, yet I still felt depressed and lonely sometimes. I started to feel like maybe I shouldn't be by myself. Maybe I was ready to date. Maybe even get married. My friends were getting married and having babies. I didn't want another baby—I already had my son— but I wanted companionship.

When I think back on it, I can't believe I was thinking that way. A relationship was the last thing I needed during that season of my life. But at the time, I didn't care. I just didn't want to be single.

I ignored that God was slowly guiding me through a much-needed emotional transformation—and I messed up the process by seeking love in all the wrong places. My fairytale idea of love, relationships, and marriage was so wrong. As a result, I ended up in countless, meaningless relationships based on sex more than anything else. I often found myself crying to the Lord at the altar because I kept doing things that weren't conducive to my spiritual growth.

I believe my mindset about being single got sidetracked for two reasons.

The first was that I thought being in a relationship would help me heal. I was lonely, and I wanted to get married.

I now understand that I was rushing the process. The Lord had started healing me and changing me, but I interrupted. I needed to sit back, relax, and let God heal Tammie, rather than Tammie trying to do it her way. "He healeth the broken in heart and bindeth up their wounds" (Psalm 147:2, KJV). I had to trust God and leave it in His hands. I had to believe that He would heal my trauma.

"Then Jesus said, come to me, all you who are weary and burdened, and I will give you rest. Take my yoke upon you and learn from me, for I am gentle and humble in heart, and you will find rest for your souls" (Matthew 11:28-29, KJV). Through prayer and devotion, I learned that Jesus could give me rest from all my troubles. I just had to leave my burdens in the Lord's hands and have faith that all will be okay.

The second reason my mindset was sidetracked was that I let my guard down. I allowed the enemy to get into my ear and plant seeds of doubt about my healing. He told me I'd always be alone and that I needed someone else to help me heal. He even said I wasn't going anywhere in the church—that they actually hated me. I started skipping services, and I stopped reading my Bible. I began to drink again. I became depressed and isolated myself from anything having to do with the Church.

I fell for his lies and deception during that time of my life—"Lest Satan should take advantage of us; for we are not ignorant of his devices" (2 Corinthians 2:11, NKJV). I was still new in Christ, and I was definitely ignorant of his devices and traps he set for me. I was so caught up in my desires—in what *I* wanted. I did not want to be single, and I was afraid to be alone. The enemy knew this and used it to his advantage to plant doubt and discouragement in my mind.

Yet again, I found myself asking God for another chance, for forgiveness for my actions. As I rebuilt my relationship with God, my way of thinking and my self-perception changed. "But ye are a chosen generation, a royal priesthood, a peculiar people: that ye should shew forth the praise of him who hath called you out of darkness into his marvelous light." (1 Peter 2:9, KJV). I finally realized that I am *somebody!*

I'm so glad that I have been spiritually adopted into a royal family, where I have access to God at any time—through prayer, worship, study of His word, and devotion. I am somebody to Him. I am valuable to Him. He is my Father, protector, healer, teacher—and my prince of peace. It feels so good to be part of a family where there is genuine love from the father. I no longer have to worry about being single, finding a relationship, or whether I'll ever get married. God knows what's best for me. He knows just what I need.

Today I embrace my singleness! I'm not sad. I'm not mad. And I don't have any regrets. Being single allows me to devote more time to my relationship with God through prayer and the study of His Word. Being a Christian single isn't a curse. It isn't a punishment for something we did in the past. Singleness has purpose. It allows us to focus on spiritual growth and goals without having to balance it with a relationship. Being single also gives you the space to grow personally by explore your own interests and passions.

My singleness has a purpose—it allows me to seek and discern my calling with clarity and intention. I will continue —and am determined—to be steadfast and immovable, always abounding in the work of the Lord, knowing that in Him, my labor is not in vain.

And the Clock Strikes Twelve

ALISON ASSANAH-CARROLL

Time—my most precious commodity—is both a blessing and a curse, a gift and a reminder. It has been the subject of innumerable reflections, notably in music. Michael Jackson reminded us to "Remember the Time." Prince warned us with "Sign O' The Times." Whitney inspired us with "One Moment in Time," and Bill Medley and Jennifer Warnes reminded us, "I've Had the Time of My Life."

As a single woman, I've waltzed through various phases of life, sidestepping the things that I want to avoid like the plague—signs of aging, the reality that I have more years behind me than I do ahead of me, and the ever-present awareness of the mortality of those I love. Even with these mind-boggling considerations, I'm thrilled by the things I've done, the things I still want to do, and the freedom of being single.

It's eight o'clock on a Friday night, and I am . . . in the house.

Hold up. Stop the press!

Yep, you read that right. Big hand on twelve, little one on eight. And Friday? I should be out painting the town red. So why am I not standing in front of the mirror, debating which outfit to wear?

Because I'm here, snuggled in my fleecy onesie covered in Snuffleupagus eyelashes—and there's not a glimmer of regret or shame to my game. Tiny as my place may be, it's my haven. And truth be told, staying home has become a revolutionary act of joy. I don't need to be at every gathering or event to feel relevant. Staying in is a choice—maybe even a statement. Posting selfies on social media might give an exhilarating high as the comments and likes pour in, but my worth isn't defined by the number of 'likes' on a party post—no matter how damn good I looked while doing it! Sometimes, being relevant is simply about being at peace with myself—and that's exactly where I am!

To know me is to understand my backstory. Who is this enigmatic soul?

I'm a single woman with passions as deep as the gorges of the Serengeti. I'm a daughter, sister, and friend. I'm a descendant of my parents' unspoken promises—the promise to create a better life for me than they had themselves, and the promise not to repeat the same mistakes their parents made with them. I am Alison Lacey Assanah-Carroll, the proud daughter of a South American father and an American mother, born in Ohio and raised in Baltimore.

My father was a brilliant man, who, despite being blind, taught chemistry to the biology and pre-med majors of the family with unparalleled precision. He balanced the equations in his head, never getting them wrong. But eventually, the blindness that dimmed his spirit, followed by the heart attack that claimed his life, took him from us.

When the clock struck six on January 13, 2010, time froze. My world shattered, and the course of my life changed forever. Despite the arsenal of words in my vocabulary, I couldn't find one to express the depth of my pain. The kind of pain that threatened to become my personal hell—one I would spend years trying to escape, and even longer trying to heal from. That moment in time robbed me of my best friend and stole my number one fan—my dad.

My mother is talented in her own right. With her natural artistic flair, she's able to do amazing things—interior design, crafting beautiful pottery, and snagging rare finds at thrift stores and vintage shops. And she gardens like she's gunning for *Better Homes and Gardens* Woman of the Year. At ninety-one, she's still living life on her own terms—and without a doubt, my determination comes from her.

My father's parents passed away before I was born, and although I would have loved to have met them, the love I received from my mother's side of the family was more than enough. My middle name, "Lacey," is a tribute to my grandfather, Lacey Flagg—and I carry his name with pride. By all accounts, he was a gentle, loving soul. He was also the brother of the renowned Margaret Flagg Holmes, one of the founding members of Alpha Kappa Alpha Sorority, Incorporated. Yes, I'm a proud legacy of the AKA's and deeply saddened by the fact that I never had the chance to pledge. Still, representing my grandpa and the remarkable family legacy behind him fills me with immense pride and joy.

My grandmother was a beautiful woman and a trailblazer, far ahead of her time. She imparted the kind of wisdom that has served me well over the years. Unbeknownst to me, I was being armed with the strength and wisdom needed for independence and singlehood.

Long before I could read, she sang recipes to the tunes of my nursery rhyme songs, making cooking a fun-filled game. As long as I did exactly what she did, our game continued. But when I made a mistake, I had to relinquish my bowls and spoons so she could rectify my faux pas. I hated giving up my cooking utensils, which perhaps explains why I'm such a foodie and enjoy cooking to this day. In hindsight, her instruction has been invaluable, particularly when it comes to my culinary skills, which definitely come in handy when fending for myself and whipping up a delicious meal for one! After all, a girl's gotta eat, right?

I attribute a significant part of my poetry-writing ability to her. As a little girl, I would lie awake at night, playing rhyming games with her. She'd toss out a phrase like, "black, black sit on a tack," and expected me to provide a comeback that rhymed with hers. Her infectious laughter filled me with so much joy, and I was never sad when she was around. The confidence and reassurance she instilled in me helped shape the woman I've become.

I took my first trip to South America when I was eleven. It was the perfect time to go to Guyana—I was old enough to appreciate the beauty of the country, and it was the trip that affirmed who I was, where I came from, and the responsibility of being an "Assanah." It was an awakening that piqued my curiosity about other places and opened my eyes to a whole world out there just waiting to be explored.

At home, expectations were high. I'm one of two girls, and as the older sister, eight years ahead, I often felt the pressure to lead by example. My sister looked up to me, sometimes holding me to standards that bordered on impossible. I wrestled with my desire for freedom and self-expression. My mother's "be home by twelve" rule felt intolerable, especially when the real fun didn't begin until midnight. I loved to dance, and Odell's was the club where I could shed my inhibitions and mingle with the who's who of Baltimore. Their tagline said it all—"You'll Know If You Belong." I certainly couldn't feel like I belonged when I had to be in by midnight, so I missed curfew, taking the subsequent punishment, so I could savor the escape that came from dance moves to house music that seemed like it would never end.

I wasn't allowed to date during high school. The primary focus in my household was education, and although I graduated with honors, my point of contention was always about curfew. I was diligent and intentional in my studies, so I felt I had earned the right to make my own decisions about when to come home. But that just wasn't happening, and I considered myself lucky to attend an outside prom at Forest Park High School, along with my own junior and senior proms. Even those permissions required negotiations that felt like brokering world peace.

My father ruled with an iron fist, and my parents held the reins tightly—factors that fueled my desire for independence and exploration. Venturing out as a single woman never scared or intimidated me. It felt like a rite of passage that liberated me.

Life was a vibrant mix of lessons in etiquette, strict rules, and occasional rebellion, but these early experiences molded me into who I am today—a woman empowered by resilience and dancing freely outside the confines of my parents' boundaries.

The natural step after high school was to pursue a college degree. But what began as a burning desire quickly began to waver. After a whirlwind year at the renowned Morgan State University, my bucket list began tugging at my heartstrings. I knew it was time to embark on my own adventure.

My parents had done their job, instilling strong morals and a sense of self-respect. With my integrity intact and a concise understanding of right from wrong neatly stored in my memory bank, I bought a plane ticket and headed to California. I had always fantasized about living in Los Angeles, and being single handed me the keys to explore it without limits.

One of my best girlfriends, Linda, and I used to set that city ablaze from sun-up to sundown. I was young, attractive, and carefree, a combination that drew attention and gained us access to the places we wanted to go. Our escapades included happy hours at the iconic Red Onion on Wilshire, late-night dancing at Osco's, Tiberio's in the ABC Entertainment Center, and Flannigan's in Marina del Rey, where DJ Julian Jackson was spinning irresistible beats.

We modeled in fashion shows throughout Los Angeles, worked as hair models for the infamous Royal Coiffures Salon, and even modeled on boat cruises to Catalina Island. We partied the nights away at the legendary Carolina West, The Speak Easy, and

Little Jays. Sunrise breakfasts at The Pantry were a staple, and we indulged at Fatburger's and Roscoe's Chicken and Waffles. We savored garlicky delights at The Stinking Rose, enjoyed the smooth jazz sounds at The Townhouse, enjoyed fantastic music at Concerts by the Sea, and attended unforgettable parties hosted by the infamous Marc Gaspar at the Roof Garden and other sexy spots in the city.

We were everywhere, doing anything and everything we wanted, living with joy and without regret. We were living single long before it was ever a television show. Life in Los Angeles was a vivid tapestry of unforgettable moments, food, and friend-ships. That is, until my father's health began to fail, making my move back to Maryland inevitable. Though I left Los Angeles behind, I'm still friends with Linda to this day—and "California Dreaming" will always be on my mind and in my heart.

Being single gave me the freedom to embark on exotic adven-tures to faraway places. One memorable trip was to the beautiful island of Trinidad. Strangely enough, fate always seemed to flirt with me during travels— and this trip was no exception. Somewhere in the cosmos, someone or something had other plans for my singlehood.

Enter Mukesh—a gorgeous Trinidadian lifeguard at Maracas Bay Beach and trainer of professional swimmers. Our ini-tial encounter was brief yet intentional, marked by his direct approach, warm introduction, and genuine interest. He wasn't crass or crude, but a true gentleman who'd noticed a woman who intrigued him.

He asked to stay in touch while I was vacationing in Trinidad so we could get to know each other. My girlfriends teased me, brushing it off as a fleeting vacation rendezvous—but Mukesh had other intentions. When I returned home from Trinidad, he called me every day for months after, proving just how serious he was. He even went as far as booking an extended holiday to the States to spend time with me.

The clock was kind to us. We took several trips together, attended a wedding, and filled our time with a variety of summertime activities, savoring every moment and etching memories in our minds. Everywhere we went, people assumed we were married, often complimenting us on what a cute couple we made.

As our relationship gained momentum, we started discussing our goals and plans for the future. Mukesh envisioned a life with me in Trinidad, as his wife, having babies and raising them on the island. And while the idea of being married to such an attractive, attentive, God-fearing man was alluring, his vision of me barefoot and pregnant didn't align with mine. I wanted to finish my college degree in the States.

This and the distance between us became the hurdles that eventually brought our relationship to a close. Like the waves crashing on the shores of Maracas Bay, our love was eventually pulled out to sea with the sand from the beach.

Age may just be a number, but the big three-zero was a momentous occasion. My freedom and independence were worth celebrating, especially knowing that, by God's grace, I would see another birthday. The Paradise Island Resort and Casino earned the honor of hosting the festivities. Passports in hand, eight of us headed to the Bahamas, swearing that "what happens in the Bahamas stays in the Bahamas."

With beautiful weather, loads of laughs, and drinks flowing freely, we were set for adventure— no excuses, no apologies. We had no one to answer to but ourselves. One day, my sister and I went from Paradise Island to the Nassau marketplace for shopping-usually an uneventful zip across the water. But fate had other plans. My sister's jet ski engine flooded, and she had to hop off in the middle of the ocean so the water could be drained. I was clinging to her for dear life, praying this wouldn't be the day we'd face an unexpected shark attack or some other ocean catastrophe.

It would have been an absolutely mortifying experience had it not been made so humorous by the rescue ranger who saved the day. He was the owner of the parasailing business on the beach, and as fate would have it, was actually named "Dexter." Now, what are the odds of that? Dexter!

Through it all, my faith has remained an unyielding anchor. It reminds me that I am loved and protected by a power far greater than myself. Loving God has taught me how to love myself. I can now enjoy my milestone moments with those who genuinely care, free from the spotlight and free from the opinions of haters. The only ones who matter are those who want to see me succeed, with no envy and no hidden agendas.

I'm blessed to be surrounded by a wonderful group of people whom I am honored to call my friends. I'm grateful to God for them every day. They've been with me through every joy, every pain. They are unique, talented, and quirky in their own right, always showing up for a good meal, a check-in call, some great drinks, or nonstop laughter.

Kenny's, "Hey, hun, whatcha doin'?" is my cue for a nice drive or a trip to Starbucks for my favorite Caramel Macchiato. Lisa greets me with her cheerful, "Hey Allie Pallie, what's shakin'?" Debbie's warm "Hey Girl" always ends with "luv you" at the end of every call. Lanette's articulate, "Hi, my friend." Sylvia's staccato baby-voiced, "Hi Alison." Mark's dignified, "Hi, sweetheart." Linda's matter-of-factly, "Hey Alison. What's going on?" And last but not least, Airuel's signature, "Yo, What's happening?" Each greeting is unique, and I look forward to hearing their voices on the other end of the line—affirming life, affirming friendship, affirming love!

I have grown to enjoy the unpredictability of a day without plans and the gift of time spent with friends when schedules permit. Sure, the clock can feel relentless, dragging without mercy during the workweek and flying like on steroids on the weekends. I often catch myself staring at the clock, wishing I could somehow stretch out the precious moments that have left me with treasured memories.

Maybe one day I'll crack the code on how to slow time down. And when I do? Look out, world! There have been countless beautiful trips and unforgettable moments when I would have loved to have been able to push pause, rewind, and freeze the moment in time.

Although being single is a choice, I give myself the grace to consider what life would be like with the right man. While my existence isn't dependent upon—or defined by—a man, I know that I could definitely enhance the life of one. Talk about your ride-or-die girl? That's me all day. If a man gives me the best of who he is, I'll mirror that and go to the mat with him and for him. We'd be a formidable team. And I'm a hopeless romantic, unapologetically allowing myself to be vulnerable if it means getting the best of what our love has to offer.

There was a moment when I decided I didn't want to be single anymore. So I went about doing what would change that narrative—I joined a dating site. And that's where I met the love of my life–a love that grew so organically it felt predestined. We met online on the final day of our dating memberships, both planning to cancel but compelled to scroll one last time. My profile caught his eye. Curiosity got the best of him, and he left me a message that said, "If you'd like to meet for a glass of wine or a cup of coffee, give me a call."

Just as I was about to push the "cancel" button, I received his notification. I opened the message and saw his profile picture. That man was so damn fine I thought I was being catfished. I waited a few days before reaching out, and when I did, it felt like reconnecting with a long-lost friend. Our nightly conversations stretched into the wee hours of the morning, but despite sleep deprivation, I was invigorated by each new day and what our next conversation would hold.

It was eight months before we met face-to-face. Our conflicting schedules—and our commitment to creating a quality relationship—became the very barriers that pushed us to get to know one another. Nothing was off limits in our conversations, allowing us to build a bond and develop the kind of trust that wrapped around us like a warm blanket on a cold winter night. Although our relationship was long-distance, he made New York seem like it was right around the corner.

When we both decided the time was right, he meticulously crafted a plan that aligned our schedules and gave us opportunities to enjoy quality time together. His dedication to making it work was evident in every detail. Like Steve Harvey famously asked in *Think Like a Man*, "Does he have a plan for you, or is he just playing with you?" Well, Eben had a plan, and he proved it every day. Not a day went by without us connecting, even if just for a moment. The respect we had for one another made it easy to make decisions beneficial to our future.

I knew I was in love when Eben showed up at my door during a medical emergency involving my kidney. He left New York amid a high-alert situation and mandatory overtime, breaking protocol to be by my side. Not only did he take me to the hospital and stay with me for hours every day, but he also managed things at home, including walking my fur baby, Mikey, several times per day. His steadfast commitment and selfless acts confirmed that he was the one for me. His honesty, care, and concern were refreshing. Even though we'd had some difficult conversations, we stood firm on the solid foundation we'd created. His presence, his warmth, his touch, and his passion gave me a safe space that allowed trust to thrive. Several weeks later, he again left me speechless when he proposed to me at the Inner Harbor. The ring was a testament to his love, but it was the words of his proposal that really swept me off my feet. Sometimes, you just know. Saying "yes" to him was as natural as breathing. He made singlehood seem like the most preposterous idea I had ever embraced.

The 11:15 a.m. call in February 2017 telling me he was gone took my breath away. Losing him was a pain so devastating it transcended universal comprehension. I dreaded weekends, reminders that our cherished commutes between New York and Baltimore were over. His death left me with more time to think about all that I'd lost. He was the perfect man—intelligent, kind, and an avid dog lover. His culinary skills rivaled any top chef, turning our dinners into a five-star dining experience. A wizard with computers and graphics software, he launched his business, RUKGRAFX, with ease. And boy, could he sing! He got that honestly- his entire family was musically inclined- shout out to Huey Dunbar and the infamous DLG family!

The cancer started in his brain and metastasized, ravaging his body without mercy. It was one of the hardest things I'd ever had to face. I was broken, lost, angry, hurt, and afraid. The emotions ran so deep they threatened to swallow me up in an abyss.

I was furious at 9/11. The aftermath of those explosions had ruined what was meant to be the greatest love story ever told.

In losing him, I lost more than just one person. I lost my best friend, my lover, my business partner, and my confidant. I needed time to grieve each loss, but my heart and mind couldn't fully accept that none of them would be there for me. There would be no more of him. And to throw more hurt onto the pain, there would be no more birthday songs. How I wish I had recorded just one of the times he sang to me for my birthday.

We always think we have more time—maybe even a lifetime. But sometimes, it's only a moment.

The love we shared changed me. I now realize that God brought him to me to show me how I should be treated in a relationship. Eben was my Boaz. And now, because of him, I can recognize the impostors when they show up in sheep's clothing.

Everything about singlehood isn't always "champagne wishes and fairytale dreams," and I'd be a fool to try to convince you otherwise. Sometimes, in the throes of being single, I get sad— especially when I think about how losing the love of my life felt like time stopped. No matter what I did, my heart wouldn't stop hurting. Self-medicating didn't help. Writing didn't help. Crying didn't help, and I couldn't pray. The blessing I had been given had been cursed with cancer, and he wasn't coming back.

Two of the most important men in my life were gone. My father in 2010 and Eben in 2017. Those tremendous losses affirmed my need for help to get through the pain.

Why is it that people shy away from that seven-letter word? (Stop counting—"single" only has six letters!) No, I am talking about **therapy**. You know, the thing that helps you to confront your demons, ease your pain, and quell your fears so you can become the best version of yourself. For me, it became a lifeline.

Therapy has been a critical part of my healing journey. My therapist made me dig deep—pushing every button I had. Love, death, childhood trauma, sex, heartbreak, illness, betrayal, work, pain—nothing was off limits! There were days I swore I'd never see him again. And in good 'ol feisty fashion, I would tell him so. But without fail, he'd calmly affirm my feelings and then softly say, "I'll see you next week."

No matter how mad or upset I was when leaving his office, I always found the strength to push through and show up for that next visit. Was it easy? Absolutely not. But the peace of mind and strength that it has given me has been priceless. Was it worth it? Absolutely! And I would do it again to ensure my ability to navigate the things that make life's journey precious and worthwhile.

Being single has taught me how to date *me*. I've come to realize that I have so many passions and interests that keep me curious and engaged. Writing is one of them—whether it's poetry, children's books, treatments for film and television, research papers, or grants—you name it, and I've done it. I also love the visual and performing arts. Most recently, I took art classes in which I created my own masks and a three-dimensional mixed-media graphic. Although far from perfect, I'm completely enamored with the fact that I stepped outside of my comfort zone to try things I've always wanted to do.

The year 2025 is already promising to be both exciting and enterprising, filled with the execution of several projects and the realization of dreams that have been deferred for far too long.

Being human, of course, I think about sex, and being single offers a tremendous amount of freedom when it comes to it. But in full transparency, as I've aged, I've come to hold it in much higher regard. I recognize its profound significance and the soul ties it creates.

I have male friends who are more than willing—eager, even—to oblige my sexual urges. But I don't want to *just* have sex. I want to be aligned with someone with whom I'm evenly yoked. When that desire is finally realized, I want it to be about making love, forging a bond that's meaningful and committed, and building a lasting relationship.

I simply don't believe God would place this kind of love in my heart without providing the right person to share it with. Sharing myself with a man is a gift, not an obligation, and not a task to check off my 'To Do' list.

Until that time—if it's ever meant to be part of my story—I'll wait for God to provide that man. One who is intentional in choosing me as opposed to me being an option. His actions will align with his words, and he will show me that we're doing this thing called life together, for better or for worse.

Trust and believe, it will take more than a honeymoon phase or the "90-Day Rule" for him to get *these* cookies. But, until then, should that time ever arrive, I'll keep doing me and enjoying all that life has to offer on this single-and-ready-to-mingle highway.

There are moments when doubts and fears creep in—because I'm human, and that's only natural. During one of those moments, a dear friend shared some sage advice— "Put your secret out there before anyone else has the chance to tell it. Take the power away from them." That wisdom taught me that there's strength in honesty and that owning my truth makes me untouchable. For that pearl, I will always be grateful.

So here's my secret.

Even though I've learned to navigate the lanes of singlehood extremely well, I am terrified of dying alone. I come from an extremely small family, and I don't have children of my own. I have many loyal and dedicated friends, but they have their own lives and their own responsibilities. And at the end of the day, the same way I came into this world will be the same way I leave it—alone.

As the clock approaches midnight and I look back on these pages that reflect the culmination of memorable moments, intimate feelings, and even some of my darkest thoughts, I'm reminded that I am all that I am. And that is enough.

My journey as a single woman has rich, full of overwhelming joy, crushing pain, and everything in between. I've faced heartbreak and found new strength. I've cried, laughed, and loved—all while embracing life on my terms.

There's no magical carriage parked outside to whisk me away. But the good news? I'm not turning into a pumpkin either.

The true magic lies in the fact that I dared to take this journey.

So, to anyone reading this who's walking a similar path, know that **you are enough**.

Being single isn't a curse. It's not a shameful scarlet letter or a death sentence. It's a choice. It's an exercise in independence. Time ticks on—and the journey is yours for the taking.

So dare to take it. Because time waits for no one.

And, as my fingers strike the last autocorrection key, I'm inspired to leave these final words:

I AM ALL THAT I AM

I am her, and she is me,
Embracing my beauty, strong, wild, and free
My heart, my soul, my silent vow,
To seize all of life and live it now.
For I'm enough just as I stand,
Enamored by life's bold, open hand.
Single but full, not lonely, not sad,
Walking my path, and for that, I am glad.

By: Alison Assanah-Carroll

With the final line written and the last sentence completed, I feel a profound sense of fulfillment. And as the clock strikes twelve, I close this chapter with a toast to myself and a sense of peace, knowing that my story has been told and that I am single, lovable, and far from sad!

Three Strikes

LARAY WILLIAMS

The term "three strikes" is usually associated with something negative. In baseball, if the batter swings and misses the flying ball three times, it's a strikeout. In legal terms, a person convicted of the same crime—often drug-related or another criminal activity—three times may face a long-term prison sentence. In almost all instances, "three strikes" leads to a negative consequence.

Well, I have a different take on the expression. I've been engaged three times. If applying the same "three strikes" logic to my situation, I should be out. But that's not my story. Each of the three engagements—and subsequent breakups—helped me mature and find my purpose.

I've written some reflections on those relationships because the true lessons are not in the details, but in the lessons learned.

Strike # 1 - Young Love

When you're young and in love, you feel like nothing can stop you—until reality hits. For me, it came in the form of a mixed family and a third child on the way. I was nineteen, and both of us were teenage parents, raising children from previous relationships. At the time, we truly believed we could conquer the world. We had our lives planned out—but we weren't ready for real life.

The relationship ended shortly after the birth of our son. Looking back, there are some things I would have done differently. First, I wouldn't have allowed other people to have a say in my relationship. Second, I would have made sure my partner and I stood firmly by the goals we had set for our relationship and family.

Even now, we're able to have respectful conversations without any ill feelings.

Strike #2 - Out of the Blue

My second engagement was all wrong. It happened decades later after the first. I was an empty nester, traveling often for work, and on one of my visits home, I reconnected with someone I had dated more than twenty years earlier.

Some people don't change—they just get more proficient at the games they play. He said all the right things, but something felt wrong from the start. We reconnected in September, and by December, he proposed. I believe I only said yes because he asked in front of my family.

That's when the red flags began to show up. The relationship was long-distance, and the significant time difference made his behavior more obvious. He'd disappear on the weekends, saying he'd lost his phone, then argue with me for the littlest thing. His timeline and things he said he did didn't line up, and I heard a different story every time we talked.

Eventually, I hired a private investigator. It didn't take long to confirm what I thought—he was seeing multiple women. His true motive for marriage was revealed during an argument about getting married, pre-marital counseling, and a prenuptial agreement. I told him I wanted a prenup. We weren't youngsters building a life together. We had separate lives and careers, and I wanted both of us to be protected. That's when he told me the reason he wanted to marry—I was smart and financially stable, and he wanted the money he assumed I had.

Laughter was the only response I could give at the time. What he didn't know was that three days before, I'd had a dream that confirmed I couldn't marry him. In the dream, I was saying "I do" when an angel fell off my shoulder and died. I woke up shaken and knew this wasn't right—it wasn't for me. That relationship ended quickly.

Later, I heard from one of his relatives. They wanted to know what had happened. I told my side of the story, and they confirmed that what I had suspected was true—and added some things I hadn't known. I was grateful I listened to my gut and followed through on ending the relationship.

Strike # 3 - Opposites Don't Attract

He called and asked, "Are you ready?"

"Yes, I'm ready," I responded.

"When are you coming home?"

"Not just yet. I have one more assignment."

A year later, he called again. "Are you coming home for the holiday?"

"Yes."

"Okay, let's do this."

We had been waiting for this moment since we first met, some forty years ago. We went to school together—he was older than I was—and though we always felt a connection, the timing was never right. We were total opposites, but we believed we were soulmates. Years earlier, we'd made an agreement—if neither one of us were married by a certain age, we'd start a relationship with the goal of marriage.

At first, it was total bliss. We talked daily discussed the future—what our goals were and how we'd accomplish them. One shared goal was to become an entrepreneurs since we were both in the same industry. During my visits, he'd pick me up from the airport no matter what part of the country he was in. We were inseparable, except when he had to leave on business—and sometimes, I would go with him.

But as the time for me to go home approached, I noticed a change in his behavior and communication. He would be short on the phone, and sometimes he wouldn't call for two days. Something didn't feel right, but I ignored the signs.

Once I got home, things just didn't add up. Overnight road trips when he'd already been on the road for five days. Arguments over the small stuff. I had invested too much this time to ignore the signs—so I started paying attention.

The breaking point came just days after my mother died. He had been very supportive—he was even a pallbearer at the funeral. But then he disappeared right after the service. I found out later that he was with another woman. When confronted with it, he denied it. That's when I started my own investigation.

I learned that he never ended his previous relationship . At that point, I thought it was over. But strike three came one night when he told me he had to make an overnight delivery. What really happened was he spent the night at a hotel—with her. I found out and planned to confront him in the morning.

Needless to say, that argument was emotional. But now, it really was over.

Now I had to heal.

In the Dugout:

The grieving process has five stages—denial, anger, bargaining, depression, and acceptance. I went through each one, but looking back, my grief was compounded. I was grieving my mother's death at the same time as my failed engagement.

During one of those stages, I cut my hair. And I don't mean just a trim—I went from hair appointments every two weeks to sitting in a barber's chair. After about a year of short hair, my sister (who tells it like it is) called me and said, "Me and Daddy been talking. It's over—get over it. You believed in a dream, and it was a nightmare. Live your purpose and grow your hair back!"

It wasn't until I forgave each of my ex-fiancés that I felt released—and that's when the true healing process began. Scripture tells us that if we expect God to forgive us, we have to forgive others. And I had a lot to be forgiven for—I put my desire for a relationship in front of my purpose and calling. I went with my feelings instead of facts.

I asked God for forgiveness and then called each ex-fiancé and had a conversation with them. The most difficult, of course, was the last. While he admitted he was wrong, he wouldn't take full responsibility. In the end, however, we came to a neutral understanding. That was five years ago.

Today, I'm where I'm supposed to be—walking in my full potential. And until God says, "Batter up!" I'll continue to live an authentic life with love, blessings, and healing. I'm definitely not bored!

Choosing Joy: A Journey Through Singleness, Faith, and Self-Love

CARRIE HALEY

Growing up in the heart of the Midwest—born in Missouri and partly raised in Kansas—I learned early the value of hard work, perseverance, and finding joy in simple things. Missouri was filled with a tremendous amount of family on both sides—loving and funny as heck. Kansas offered wide-open spaces where the sky seemed to go on forever and people with a kind of grit that spoke straight to the soul.

I grew up in poverty, surrounded by challenges that shaped me into someone who values resilience and determination. Life wasn't easy, and the darkness of those early years carried with it struggles that seemed to cling to my spirit long after I left those neighborhoods. Still, those same experiences sowed the seeds of profound empathy, especially for those, like me, who have been marginalized due to their intersectional identities. That

understanding has become a core part of who I am today—a woman who is unapologetically Christian, anchored by the strength and comfort my faith has given me.

It was in those same flatlands that I experienced my first relationship— a toxic, abusive one, but also where I decided I was worth saving. I began a journey that would take me through military service, marriage, motherhood, and eventually, a divorce that shattered one world and opened the door to possibilities I never imagined.

Now, here I am, 59 years old, standing in the sweet spot where freedom meets wisdom, and wisdom finally knows how to savor simplicity and joy. I've come to cherish the peace of singleness, even as I acknowledge the occasional pangs of loneliness or fleeting desire for companionship. But the beauty of this chapter of my life is that I've grown into a woman who refuses to settle. After navigating the tumultuous waters of divorce and doing the work of self-discovery, therapy, and faith, I know what I bring to the table. And I've learned that I'd rather eat alone than dine with someone who doesn't appreciate the feast of my spirit.

Divorce: A Doorway to Rediscovery

The world often paints being single as void or a space of lacking, waiting to be filled by a partner. But my journey after divorce has been anything but empty. It's been a time of profound self-discovery, spiritual renewal, and a deeper appreciation for the love I give and receive in ways that don't always fit the traditional romantic mold. My path, shaped by a deep love for Christ, has been marked by acts of service and moments of quality time that speak to the heart in ways words often fail to express.

When I walked away from my marriage, many saw it as the end of something. But for me, it was the beginning—a doorway to rediscovering myself. Divorce isn't easy, and it's not something anyone hopes for, but sometimes it's the necessary step toward reclaiming your own story. It gave me the chance to reconnect with the woman I was before marriage and to discover the version of myself that had grown stronger through life's battles.

And those battles? Oh, I've had my share. I've felt the sting of being marginalized —for my skin tone, my gender, and my economic background. As a dark-skinned Black woman, an enlisted soldier turned Army Warrant Officer (now retired), and a senior professional in the federal government, I've walked into rooms where I had to prove I belonged before I could even take a seat.

Those experiences shaped me, but they didn't break me. Instead, they made me a fierce advocate, for myself and others. They made me a woman whose heart beats for service. Through it all, I often navigated with God in the driver's seat.

Acts of Service: The Way I Speak Love

To know me is to understand that acts of service are my love language. It's how I pour my heart out—whether I'm volunteering, mentoring, or simply offering a shoulder to lean on. I think back to my time in the military, stationed in places like Germany, Korea, and Bahrain, or traveling for leisure to Italy, Ghana, and Egypt. In each of those places, I saw that the need to serve isn't bound by borders. It's a universal calling, one that speaks to our shared humanity.

Leaning into who I am as a human and how I express my love through acts of service hasn't always been easy, especially in relationships. Some partners didn't want me to travel without them. Others lacked the means to go with me. Some resented my generosity to others in need. But what they saw as a flaw drew me closer to God. My inclination to serve strengthened my relationship with Him. My faith is the cornerstone of my life, my rock in turbulent times, my comfort in solitude.

I love Christ without hesitation and see His mercy and grace in the simplest things every day—the breath that moves through my nostrils to my lungs, the morning sun kissing my face, hysterical laughter about nothing, and morning texts from family and friends to see how I'm doing. Through Christ, I've learned that serving others is one of the highest forms of love. But I've also learned something equally important—service starts with taking care of myself.

Self-Care: A Radical Act of Love

For a long time, I thought self-care was a luxury. Growing up in the Midwest, where we valued community over individual needs, taking time for myself often felt selfish. But I've come to understand what *The Best Investment is Within One's Self*

(2nd ed.) puts so well— "Self-care is not just an indulgence; it's a radical act of self-love. It's a way of telling myself that I am worthy and that my needs and desires matter."

Self-care looks different now than it did while in the throes of a demanding marriage and raising children. Today, it means setting healthy boundaries, enjoying a solo dinner at one of my favorite restaurants, or retreating into the quiet of my home with a good book. It's about going to therapy and unpacking the baggage of my past. Erykah Badu's *Bag Lady* comes to mind—I was still dragging the weight of my past, unable to face the pain I had stuffed into the recesses of my mind, like the trauma of sexual assault and the mental anguish and physical abuse that had left me feeling invisible and voiceless.

Self-care is also about honoring my love for travel—for cultural immersion and seeing with my own eyes what others only read about in books. Whether walking the packed streets of Tokyo or standing on the shores of the Gold Coast in Barbados, travel reminds me that there is a vast, gorgeous world out there—and I am an integral part of it. It's where I find new perspectives, deepen my gratitude, and reclaim my joy. Sometimes it's also where I forgive—freeing myself so I can move forward and heal.

Thank God I was able to find friendship again my ex-husband— someone I know I can rely on and share my concerns with, and someone who remains committed to co-parenting our four children.

The Joy and Loneliness of Solitude

Of course, even the strongest among us have moments when solitude feels more like a burden than a blessing. There are nights when the silence is deafening—when I long for the warmth of another body beside me, someone to share the little details of my day. I'm human, after all. The desire for intimate connection is woven into the fabric of who we are. We are communal by design, but that doesn't always mean physical intimacy. For me, those moments of longing are fleeting—passing clouds in an otherwise clear sky. They come and go, but they don't define me.

What defines me is the decision to hold out for something real— something meaningful. I'd rather wait than settle because I know I'm worth the wait. Years of relationships not blessed by God but reasoned by me taught me that true, authentic love cannot be rushed. Bad decisions only bring more trauma and heartache. So I've learned to enjoy my own company. I savor the stillness of nights in bed, Saturday mornings spent in meditation, and Sunday afternoons curled up with a journal—reflecting on how far I've come and the peace I've found along the way.

In my book *The Best Investment is Within One's Self* (2nd ed.), I reflect on the power of meditation as a tool for decluttering the mind. Meditation is like a mental reset—a quiet invitation to pause, breathe, and release the noise that accumulates in the corners of our thoughts. Meditation creates space for peace and clarity to flourish. When we clear the mental clutter, we open ourselves to deeper self-awareness, grounding us in the present moment and allowing joy to rise from within.

In solitude, this practice becomes even more profound. It sharpens our ability to listen to our inner voice, to reconnect with our most authentic selves. What feels like loneliness is transformed into an opportunity to cultivate growth, healing, and joy.

Quality Time: Nurturing My Own Heart

Quality time is my second love language, and while it's often associated with spending time with others, I've found a way to turn it inward. For me, quality time with myself means going for long walks, letting my thoughts wander through memories of growing up in the Midwest—where fields stretched as far as the eye could see, and summers were spent beneath a sun that seemed to bless even the simplest joys. It's a chance to reconnect with that girl who once dreamed of faraway places and found solace in books and stories when the world felt too harsh to face.

And then there's the time I spend with family—my anchor, my constant reminder that I am never truly alone. These are the kind of relationships where we laugh until our sides hurt, cry without fear of judgment, and sit in comfortable silence, knowing we are deeply loved. Being single doesn't mean being isolated. It means that the love I cherish comes from places deeply rooted in history, connection, and shared experiences.

Faith: My Compass Through It All

My love for Christ has been a constant staple through every chapter of my life. It has sustained me through the darkest nights and renewed my hope when I felt like the world had written me off. In my Bible, I find reminders that my worth isn't tied to a relationship or status —it's rooted in the truth that I am fearfully and wonderfully made. My peace comes from passages like Jeremiah 29:11— *"For I know the plans I have for you, declares the Lord, plans to prosper you and not to harm you, plans to give you hope and a future."* These words have carried me through countless trials, reminding me that even when my life didn't go according to my plans, God's plans were always greater than my fears.

My relationship with Christ is intimate and personal. It's not just something I do on Sundays—it's my daily compass. It shapes how I love myself and how I show love to others, for I am commanded to love others as I love Christ. It's what gives me the strength to stand firm in my truth, singleness, and divine happiness—knowing I am never truly alone because God is always with me.

Embracing the Freedom of Singleness

There's a kind of liberation in being single that's hard to put into words. I wake up each day knowing that my time is my own—and I can spend it in ways that feed my spirit. That freedom fuels my passions, especially my lifelong love for education. Whether reading a new book on psychology or attending a class or workshop, I've always been drawn to the idea that there's more to learn and more ways to grow.

That love for learning has taken me far—both literally and figuratively. It's taken me into classrooms around the world, where

I've been both student and teacher. It reminds me that growth never ends, and that I am still becoming. In this season of my life, I'm deeply grateful to have found joy in knowing I am exactly where I'm meant to be.

I may not have all the answers, and I may not have a partner, but I have peace. And I have love—love for God, love for my family, and love for myself. That's everything I need to be happy. And if, later in my journey, I do find a blessed relationship—my Boaz—I will be ready, emotionally mentally, and spiritually, to step into it.

Conclusion: A Life of Fullness, a Life of Choice

I sometimes wrestle with what it truly means to be single—to embrace this journey with all its highs and lows. It means choosing joy, even when loneliness knocks at the door. It means holding out for a love that's worth the wait, one that doesn't require me to shrink or compromise who I am to fit someone else's idea of what I should be.

It means loving Christ and allowing His love to shape how I move through the world—how I serve, how I care for myself, and how I embrace the freedom that singleness offers. It's knowing that I am enough, just as I am. My life, my story, and my journey have value—not because of who stands beside me, but because of who I am when I stand alone.

And it's in this beautiful, messy, joy-filled space that I have discovered agape, the truest, most enduring form of love—the love that comes from within.

The Upside of Divorce: This Is What Power Looks Like

MARY MURRILL

Embracing the Single Life

After my divorce, I found myself in a place I had never prepared for, even though I knew it was coming. My son was heading off to college, and suddenly, the house was empty. A place once filled with laughter, chaos, and all the noise that comes with family life was now quiet. For the first time, I had to think about what the next chapter of my life would look like.

For so long, I had defined myself by my roles as a wife and mother. My world revolved around family, caring for everyone else and supporting my ex-husband in our joint ventures. Now, I was faced with a new reality. I needed to rediscover who I was outside of the roles I'd lived in for so many years.

Initially, it was a struggle. I had no idea where to begin. I had been so immersed in family life that I'd neglected to nurture my

own passions and aspirations. But I began to see that this was my opportunity for change. A chance to embrace my independence and figure out who I was, what I loved, and what I was capable of doing.

Even though the future felt uncertain, I didn't want to let fear hold me back. I knew that God had a plan for me, and that by trusting him, I would discover my true purpose and live the life ordained for me. I chose to step into this new season with faith and hope, believing that my best years weren't behind me, they were ahead of me.

Stepping Into Entrepreneurship

As I began exploring new opportunities, I reflected on the skills I had acquired over the years. Working with my father in his construction business taught me a great deal about running a business. I handled administrative tasks, managed projects, and learned how to keep everything running smoothly. Later, during my marriage, my ex-husband and I launched a limousine company. I took on a similar role there, overseeing back-end operations like website maintenance, graphic design, payroll, and accounting.

When I found myself single again, I realized I already had a solid foundation of skills that could support a business of my own. I knew how to manage and organize, and I had a passion for creativity and problem-solving. That's when I decided to become a virtual assistant.

I spent a lot of time researching what it meant to be a virtual assistant, how to structure it as a business, and which services to offer. I discovered that many small businesses, especially startups, needed help with administrative support and website design. My experience with website building and graphic design was a perfect fit for this market. I began reaching out to other limousine companies and small businesses, offering my services to help streamline operations and improve their online presence.

As I worked with clients, I started to notice a growing demand for website design. Many businesses, especially startups, struggled to create and maintain their own websites. It reminded me of my own challenges when we first launched our limousine business and needed a website. I remember the frustration of waiting for updates from our web designer, only to be ignored. Once the site was finally up and running, it was nearly impossible to get them to return a call for even the simplest updates.

That experience pushed me to learn how to update and maintain the website myself. So when I saw the opportunity to shift my focus to web design, I took it. I was eager to help others avoid the same frustrations I had faced. The transition from virtual assistant to web designer was an easy transition, and more lucrative. I found myself enjoying the creative process of building websites and supporting small businesses in establishing an online presence.

A Leap of Faith

At this point, my business was growing, but I knew I wanted to take my skills and knowledge to the next level. Despite some hesitation, I decided to pursue a degree in business administration with a concentration in marketing at Strayer University. Going back to school wasn't something I had planned for. I was a lot older, and the idea of being a student again felt intimidating. But I believed it was the right move, and I was determined to prove to myself that I could do it.

I was both excited and nervous. The idea of balancing school, my business, and my personal life was overwhelming at times, but I was determined not to let anything stop me. The classes were informative but challenging, and there were moments when I questioned my decision. But I knew that this was an investment in my future.

Graduating was one of the proudest moments of my life. I still remember going across that stage, shaking the professor's outstretched hand, and receiving my diploma as my family and friends cheered me on. It wasn't just a personal victory; it was a victory for every woman who's ever doubted their ability to chase something big. I was the first to come out from behind the curtain that day, and hearing the applause confirmed that I had finished what I set out to do. I had completed a major life goal and proven to myself that it was never too late to pursue my dreams.

Graduating with honors, as a cum laude student, filled me with pride. It was a testament to my perseverance and my belief that anything is possible when you trust in yourself and follow through with hard work and determination.

Overcoming Fear

I remember when I received an invitation to share my story of going through a divorce as a Christian woman. At first, I worried about what others might think of me and whether I was truly ready to be vulnerable. Divorce is often seen as a failure, and I wasn't sure I wanted to share my personal pain with others. But someone encouraged me, and deep down, I knew my story had the potential to help others facing similar struggles. So I took a deep breath and agreed.

I wrote about the emotional highs and lows and the strength I found through faith and perseverance. What I didn't anticipate was how therapeutic the process would be. As I wrote, I found myself beginning to heal even more, and I realized that vulnerability is not a weakness, but strength.

That experience led to something unexpected, I became a published author. I had contributed to an anthology, and my story was now out in the world. I was terrified at first, but at my first book signing, as I autographed copies and spoke with guests, I realized just how powerful it was to share my truth. And it wasn't just empowering for me; it gave hope to others navigating the challenges of divorce.

Stepping Into Leadership

As I continued to grow in confidence, another opportunity came my way, I was asked to teach a Bible study class. My first reaction was disbelief. Me? Teach a class? There were so many others who seemed more qualified. Even though I had been in church for years and had the knowledge, the idea of teaching scared me.

But despite my fears, I said yes. It was my first time teaching a class, and my first time using Zoom as an instructor. I had only used it before as a participant. The thought of managing the chat while trying to teach felt overwhelming, but I knew I couldn't let fear hold me back.

The first class made me nervous, but as I began to teach, I realized how much I had grown. I wasn't just teaching others; I was learning to trust in my own abilities. The experience pushed me far beyond my comfort zone, and over time, I became more confident. I realized that I could inspire and empower others through teaching.

Building Relationships

Writing my second anthology opened the door to even more opportunities. I met incredible women who were also sharing their stories and making a difference. One of the connections I made through that experience introduced me to the American Business Women's Association (ABWA), an organization dedicated to supporting and empowering women in business. I joined

ABWA and quickly became involved in several committees. The more I connected with like-minded women, the more I realized I was capable of so much more than I had ever imagined.

After three years as a member, I decided to run for vice president, and to my surprise, I won. This was a huge step for me. I was now in a leadership role, surrounded by women who were driven, successful, and passionate about their careers. Being part of ABWA opened my eyes to the power of connection and networking, and it helped me see that there are no limits to what I can achieve.

Serving with Purpose

Through my involvement with ABWA, I was introduced to Equipment Connections for Children, a nonprofit organization that loans durable medical equipment to families with young children with physical disabilities. When I was asked to serve on their board of directors, I enthusiastically accepted. It was my first time serving on a nonprofit board, and I was honored to be part of an organization making such a meaningful, tangible difference in the lives of children and their families.

Two years into my service, the executive director approached me with an exciting opportunity. He asked if I would consider becoming board president. It was a tremendous honor, and after thoughtful consideration, I accepted. Serving as board president has been one of the most rewarding experiences of my life. It has taught me the importance of giving back and making a difference in the community.

Embracing the Journey

As I look back on this incredible journey, I'm filled with gratitude. I've faced challenges, conquered fears, and accomplished things I never imagined possible. Most importantly, I've learned that my worth is not defined by my relationship status or any external circumstance. My value comes from who God created me to be.

I now understand that life is about growth, embracing change and trusting the journey, even when it's difficult. I'm more confident now than I've ever been, and I'm excited about what the future holds. With faith, perseverance, and a willingness to step out of my comfort zone, I know I'm capable of even greater things.

You Are Not Alone

To every woman reading this, know that you are not alone. Whether you are single, divorced, or navigating one of life's many transitions, remember that your story is still being written. It's okay to step back and rediscover who you are. It's okay to pursue your dreams, even if they seem impossible. You have strength, resilience, and purpose already within you, more than enough to overcome any obstacle and create a life filled with joy and fulfillment.

Keep believing in yourself. Keep moving forward. And always remember that God has a plan for your life. The best is yet to come.

Alone at Last

KIMMOLY LABOO

At the age of 47, I walked into my new luxury apartment in Kapolei, Hawaii, alone at last. Everything was pristine. The rental agent beamed as she told me I was the first to occupy the unit. It had beautiful cherry wood cabinets, hardwood floors, and a new washer and dryer. The smell of fresh paint lingered in the air, and there was a cute basket on the island with a tag that said, *Welcome Home.*

There were a lot of firsts happening in my life at that time. It was my first time living outside the state of Maryland, my first time being in Hawaii—and not just visiting but *living* there. Things were looking up. I was going through my third divorce—yes, I've been married three times. I've written about all of them in previous books, so I won't go into extensive detail here. But here's the condensed version.

At seventeen, I left home and I lived with my boyfriend and his family for a brief stint. That was a disaster.

Eventually, we got our own place—another disaster. It was an abusive situation that I quickly escaped. Thank God my cousin, who was much older, took me in until I could stand on my own two feet. During that time, I met my first husband. We moved in together, then got engaged, married, bought a home, and had two kids. We later divorced.

About three years later—I think, the timeline's a little fuzzy—I purchased a home for me and my sons. A friend who was visiting noticed the gorgeous man next door and suggested I should take notice. Well, I did—and I fell madly in love with him. We dated for six months, and he asked me to marry him several times. I was hesitant because of past trauma, but I eventually gave in. We got married, rented out his house, and lived in mine.

Shortly after we were married, he became seriously ill and was hospitalized for a long time. At home, I became his caregiver. It was one of the most difficult seasons of my life, but I was in it for the long haul. *Till death do us part,* right? Until one day, at his mother's urging, he decided to move back in with her and left me and the kids. He said it was temporary—but I made it permanent. I was devastated. We lost nearly everything, including both houses. It was a mess, and at that point, I was done—done with men, done with dating, and even done with flirting. My skirts were down to my ankles, and turtlenecks were my top of choice. I just wanted to be left alone.

About six years later, I met my third husband. We dated for three years. I wanted to date him through every season to make sure I was getting it right this time. *Third time's the charm,* right?

Wrong. We got married, purchased a home—and the relationship was a disaster from the day we moved in. I left that horrible situation six years later.

After ending my third and *final* marriage. I moved into a three-bedroom apartment with my sons. My oldest was on a break from college, and my youngest was still in high school. I didn't know what was next, but I *knew* the newfound peace was something I wanted to last.

About a year and a half later, I was hired for a position in Hawaii. I talked to my sons about it. My oldest decided to stay in Maryland, and my youngest wanted to come with me. He had applied to his dream school in California and was waiting to hear back. If I recall correctly, he graduated on a Wednesday, and we were wheels-up that Friday. My car and most of our belongings had already been packed and shipped. Soon after we arrived in Hawaii, he received the exciting news—he'd been accepted into college in Los Angeles.

On the college's move-in day, we flew to L.A., rented a car, and went shopping for essentials. We got him settled, and then it was time for me to go. I shed some tears and headed back to the airport. Five hours later, I was back home in my swanky apartment in Hawaii.

I remember standing in the kitchen thinking, *Wow—we actually did this!* It was the first time in a long time that I was genuinely happy. Home was quiet and beautiful and I was alone. No kids, no husband, just me and my thoughts. *Happy* thoughts. I didn't have to cook if I didn't want to. I didn't have to gauge someone else's mood when I entered the house. It was calm. It was easy. I wanted this feeling of peace and happiness to last forever.

During those three years in Hawaii, I took the time to figure out who I was and what I enjoyed. I tried everything—jet skiing, parasailing, hiking, luaus, whale watching, and quiet time at the beach watching gorgeous sunsets. At my youngest son's suggestion, I even drove for Lyft for a while. He thought it would be a great way for me to meet people, learn the island, and discover all the cool spots. He was right—I loved it. It's not something I'd do anywhere else, but in Hawaii, nearly everyone was on vacation and happy. While living there, I also launched my publishing company. I believe it was the peace and clarity of thought—being able to hear God clearly—that made all the difference.

When I moved back to Maryland, I brought that peace and happiness with me. My oldest son told me he'd never seen me as happy as when I was living in Hawaii, and he didn't want me to lose that. I was determined not to. I am still single. Still alone. But not lonely.

I don't feel like I'm missing anything. I have a few great friends, and every once in a while, we'll go out to eat, catch a movie, or travel. But I never hesitate to do those things alone if they aren't available. I love my own company.

I don't know if I'll ever be in a relationship again. It's not something I'm opposed to. But I'm also not longing for it. I've been alone for nine years now, and I've grown accustomed to it. When I see happy married couples, I'm happy for them. When I see couples who aren't so happy—and I can spot them a mile away—I wish them peace.

Now, for those of you who may be wondering, *What about sex, companionship, intimacy?* I can honestly say that I don't miss sex at all. I know—shocking! But I'm one of those people who can't separate sex from emotion. For me, it's so much more than just a physical act. I've spent years ridding myself of those soul ties. I'd rather just leave well enough alone. For now, the Sleeping Beauty is at rest. If at some point I should hear the audible voice of God telling me he has the perfect mate for me—because I'm pretty sure that's what it would take—perhaps those things will awaken again. But until then, I'm good.

If you're in a season of singleness and finding it hard to embrace, know this—your life is not on hold, and you are not incomplete. You are whole, chosen, and deeply loved by God right now. Not someday. Not "when." *Now.*

Singleness isn't a punishment. It's a purposeful season—one where God can pour into you, heal you, strengthen you, and prepare you for what's next. Psalm 16:11 reminds us, *"In Your presence is fullness of joy."* Let that truth anchor your heart. Lean into this time. God hasn't forgotten you—He's developing you.

You are not alone.

You are becoming.

Love & Blessings,

Kimmoly

50 Things Happily Single Women Do With Their Time

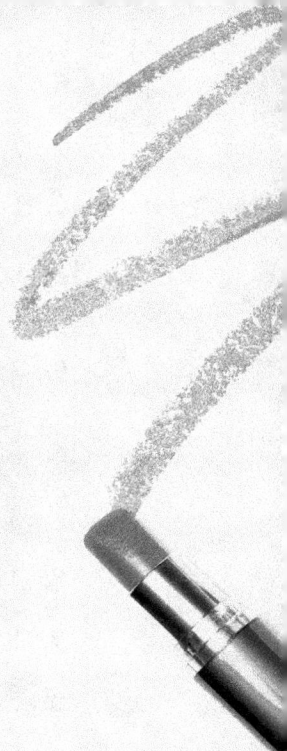

1. Travel solo or with friends

2. Take long, uninterrupted bubble baths

3. Write in journals or blogs

4. Grow in their faith and spiritual life

5. Learn a new language

6. Start a business

7. Binge-watch their favorite shows

8. Dance in their living room

9. Take themselves on dinner dates

10. Host game nights

11. Sleep diagonally in bed

12. Decorate their home exactly how they want

13. Go to therapy or coaching sessions

14. Read tons of books

15. Go on nature walks or hikes

16. Start passion projects

17. Try new recipes or take cooking classes

18. Volunteer for causes they care about

19. Say "yes" to spontaneous adventures

20. Spend quality time with family and nieces/nephews

21. Take photography walks and capture everyday beauty

22. Get regular massages or facials

23. Save and invest money wisely

24. Attend women's retreats or conferences

25. Redecorate their home just for fun

26. Take naps without guilt

27. Travel without needing permission or compromise

28. Learn how to fix things around the house

29. Create art or DIY crafts

30. Speak on stages or panels

31. Take dance or fitness classes

32. Mentor younger women or girls

33. Buy themselves flowers

34. Listen to empowering podcasts

35. Join book clubs or writing groups

36. Set goals and crush them

37. Take sabbaticals or intentional rest days

38. Explore new cities or museums

39. Post affirmations on their mirror

40. Change careers or go back to school

41. Create vision boards

42. Laugh—hard, loud, and often

43. Build strong friendships

44. Host brunches and celebrations

45. Sing in the car like nobody's watching

46. Take control of their schedule

47. Speak kindly to themselves

48. Celebrate milestones big and small

49. Dream bigger without limits

50. Enjoy their own company—and love it

About the Authors

Tamlyn L. Johnson

Tamlyn L. Johnson is a compassionate grief coach, speaker, and writer dedicated to inspiring others to live with grace, confidence, and joy. With a background in business, engineering management, and training, she brings a unique blend of wisdom, resilience, and faith to her work.

Having overcome personal challenges—including bankruptcy, divorce, and profound loss—Tamlyn has rebuilt her life with strength and purpose. She now writes, speaks, and creates uplifting, faith-centered, and inspirational content for those navigating grief, helping them find hope and joy without guilt.

Tamlyn is a grandmother, mother of five, and angel mom to one. Tamlyn understands the profound impact of loss on families and the unique challenges that come with raising children while grieving. She combines personal experience with professional expertise to create a safe and nurturing space for her clients, empowering them to honor their loved ones while moving forward with resilience and grace.

Living in Maryland, Tamlyn enjoys spending time with her family, traveling, and finding joy in everyday moments. She embraces her role as a mentor, friend, and faith-driven guide, committed to positively impacting the lives of those she serves.

Tammie Thacker

A native of Mamaroneck, New York, and now residing in Port Chester, Tammie Thacker is a devoted mother to two children, Thomas and Jasmine, and a proud grandmother to three grandsons—Bentley, Domonik, and Brixton.

She earned a Bachelor of Business Administration from Monroe University in New Rochelle, followed by an Applied Associate degree in Respiratory Care from Westchester Community College in Valhalla. With nearly three decades of experience in the respiratory field, her expertise spans adult critical care, pediatrics, and long-term care. During the COVID-19 pandemic, she served on the front lines, caring for critically ill patients requiring mechanical ventilation and advanced medical support.

For more than thirty years, she has been an active member of The Church of the Living God, Inc., serving in a variety of roles including usher/nurse president, praise and worship team member, adult Sunday School teacher, president of the Pastor-aide ministry, and currently as overseer of the Ministerial Council. She also serves as the national nurse ministry president for the denomination.

Her theological training includes certificates in Evangelism and General Bible I & II from Manhattan Bible Institute, as well as a Bachelor of Theology and Church Administration from Dominion Theological Seminary. She is on track to receive her Master of Christian Education in June 2025.

In addition to ministry and healthcare, Tammie holds certifications in Grief and Loss Counseling and Anger Management. She finds joy in studying and teaching the Word of God and enjoys watching tennis, football, basketball, and baseball in her leisure time.

Alison Assanah-Carroll

Alison Assanah-Carroll, born to a South American father and an American mother, is a native Baltimorean whose diverse background has been a cornerstone to her success. Early on, she aspired to attend Morgan State University, following in the footsteps of her parents. Enrolling in the fall of 1992, Alison graduated in just three years with a bachelor's degree in social work, achieving Summa Cum Laude honors. She continued her education at the University of Maryland at Baltimore, where she obtained a master's degree in social work and a master's Certification in Community Organization and Social Administration within a year, both with the highest honors.

Alison's remarkable talent has enabled her to introduce opportunities and create visions that span the country. She has developed several programs, including the Creative Choices

Program in California, and written grants for various organizations. Her professional experience is equally impressive. She has served as a Clinical Social Worker in the Adoptions Division of the Los Angeles County Department of Children and Family Services, where she successfully placed more than 55 wards of the state into permanent homes. She has diligently worked in Philadelphia and Maryland to preserve the well-being of causes surrounding youth and diversity, holding positions as Executive Director of the Legislative Black Caucus of Maryland, Assistant Regional Census Manager of Partnership and Data Services, Decennial Census Manager for all of Baltimore City , and Program Manager for the Youth Empowerment Program at Baltimore City Community College. Her passion for medicine and healthcare afforded her the opportunity to work as a Clinical Research Coordinator for the National Institutes of Health, where she managed and tracked 11 pediatric and 15 adult disease-specific patient populations while managing Phase II clinical trials for Fabry's Disease. Alison also served as the Genetic Research Coordinator of Genetics for the National Institute on Aging, National Institutes of Health, where she coordinated 15 genetics clinical trials for disease-specific populations with Achondroplasia, Marfan's Syndrome, Ehlers-Danlos, and short stature syndrome.

Alison's has been a contributing publisher for the article, "Echocardiographic findings in Classical and Hypermobile Ehlers-Danlos Syndromes." She is published in the International Employee Assistance Program Yearbook, Vol.1. Ed. Dale Masi, Detroit: Performance Research for "Russian and EAP's", and she holds a publication in Shadows and Light-The National Library of Poetry for her poem, "The Wishing Well." Alison was also awarded special acknowledgement for_the development of the medical manuscript that enabled the article, _"Normal Intelligence and Social Interactions in a Male Patient Despite the Deletion of NLGN4X and the VCX Genes by F. Mochel et al to be submitted for publication in the   European Journal of Medical Genetics.

Alison's consulting career began in 2001 when she was asked to review and consult on proposals submitted to the National Campaign Against Youth Violence (NCAYV) for the development of anti-violence youth campaigns, an initiative created by President Bill and Hillary Clinton, out of needs identified during the White House Conference Against Youth Violence. This role led her to managing the campaign offices and further spread her expertise in business development and grant writing. She has since assisted numerous clients aiming to start or enhance for-profit or non-profit businesses in achieving their entrepreneurial dreams.

Alison has passions that extend far beyond her professional life that include being an avid dog lover. She enjoys reading, writing, cooking, traveling; thrift store shopping, arts and crafts; and developing grants and business plans for aspiring entrepreneurs.

Laray Williams

Sometimes life's unexpected turns can challenge us to rise above our circumstances and chart a new path to success. LaRay M. Williams knows this truth intimately. At just sixteen, she became a single parent—an experience that placed her in uncharted territory and ignited a determination to overcome every obstacle in her way.

Today, she is a proud mother of two, lovingly known as "Nannan" to her grandchildren and great-niece. Her journey is a testament to perseverance, faith, and the power of community.

LaRay is a four-time graduate of the University of Maryland Global Campus, holding two Bachelor of Science degrees in Human Resources and Management Studies, an Associate of Arts in Human Resources, and a professional certificate in

Human Resources. She credits her achievements to her unwavering trust in God, the steadfast support of her parents, and the village that God faithfully placed in her life.

Beyond her academic and professional accomplishments, LaRay is an avid reader, passionate traveler, and enthusiastic baker. She actively serves her local church, where she leads the Women's Ministry and teaches Bible Study. Her heart for service also extends to Partners in Care, where she volunteers her time to support others in meaningful ways.

A dedicated mentor to young women and a woman of faith, LaRay continues to live a life of purpose, resilience, and grace— one that inspires those who have the privilege of knowing her.

Dr. Carrie Register-Haley

Dr. Carrie Register-Haley, the Founder and CEO of Revelation of Investment Coaching (roi-coaching.com) in Alexandria, VA, brings a unique approach to her role as a Certified Professional Coach from the Institute for Professional Excellence in Coaching (iPEC). Specializing in Executive and Leadership Development Coaching, Dr. Haley's method is centered on re-energizing, re-empowering, and rediscovering a passion for what you want to accomplish. Her ultimate goal is to partner with clients to explore how to discover the best version of themselves.

Dr. Haley's qualifications and experience are extensive, further underlining her expertise. She holds a PhD in General Psychology from Capella University, a Master's in Human Relations from Oklahoma University, and a range of certifications, including Myers Briggs Type Indicator, EQ-I Certified, 5 Languages of

Appreciation Facilitator, and a graduate from Federal Executive Institute. She has also obtained several certifications from Cornell University. She is enrolled in the Women's Studies Graduate Certificate Program at Howard University. Dr. Haley also served nearly 21 years of active duty in the US Army before retiring as a Chief Warrant Officer Three and continued her service to our nation in positions in the federal government.

Dr. Haley is the author of *The Best Investment is Within One's Self 2nd Edition,* available on Amazon. She has also presented empowerment workshops and keynotes to several government agencies. In the community, she serves as a key committee member for Fairfax County, Black Mental Health: Safe Place to Dig Deep; National Coalition of 100 Black Women, Inc., Northern Virginia Chapter, Past Health Committee Chair, and the Heart to Serve Ministry, Alfred Street Baptist Church. She is currently in the Health Care Ambassador position with the Buffy Foundation. Each opportunity has allowed her to experience a deeper appreciation for holistic self-discovery and Executive Leadership Empowerment Coaching.

Mary Murrill

Mary is a passionate businesswoman, creative website designer, and marketer dedicated to helping small businesses grow and succeed. With a firm belief that small businesses are the backbone of our economy, Mary leverages her expertise to help entrepreneurs generate more leads, build a strong online presence, and turn their vision into reality.

In recognition of her outstanding contributions and leadership, she has been awarded the **2025-2026 American Business Women of the Year** for the **Maryland Capital Chapter** of the American Business Women's Association (ABWA).

With a degree from Strayer University and years of hands-on experience, Mary combines creative innovation with strategic thinking to create appealing websites that perform exceptionally.

Her commitment to continuous learning and growth fuels her enthusiasm to stay prominent in marketing and design trends.

Mary is also a bestselling author with four published books, three of which have landed on national bestseller lists, focused on inspiring and empowering women. Her dedication to service extends far beyond business. She currently serves in leadership at her church, Set The Captives Free Outreach Center, and is the President of the Board of Directors at Equipment Connections for Children, a nonprofit that connects families of children with disabilities to critical adaptive equipment.

In her role as Vice President of the Maryland Capital Chapter of ABWA, Mary leads initiatives, supports recruitment, and helps drive the organization's mission to "provide women with opportunities to grow personally and professionally through leadership, education, networking, and national recognition." The organization brings together businesswomen from diverse backgrounds and occupations to support each other's development.

When she's not designing, leading, or writing, Mary loves exploring new restaurants, traveling, watching movies, networking with fellow professionals, and spending quality time with her family and friends.

Kimmoly LaBoo
VISIONARY AUTHOR

Kimmoly LaBoo is an accomplished speaker, award-winning publisher, author of eighteen books, and Certified Master Life Coach dedicated to helping others unlock their potential. As the founder and CEO of LaBoo Publishing Enterprise, she leads with care, compassion, and a clear mission: to guide independent authors through every step of the publishing journey. Her company, recognized for its excellence and innovation, has received multiple accolades for its transformative work in the literary space.

With more than a decade of experience in the publishing industry, Kimmoly has become a trusted voice and leader—empowering aspiring writers to recognize their brilliance and boldly share their stories with the world. Through her dynamic workshops, keynote speeches, and personalized coaching, she has inspired audiences across the globe to pursue purpose, live with intention, and bring their creative visions to life.

As host of *Write the Book TV*, she amplifies the voices of both emerging and established authors, offering them a vibrant platform to share their writing journeys and demystify the publishing process. Her impact extends beyond the screen, having been featured on Think Tech Hawaii, WPB Networks, Heaven 600 radio, ABC2News, and FOX5 News.

Kimmoly has spoken on stages both nationally and internationally, including the Global Literacy Conference in Ghana, the U.S. Department of Veterans Affairs, Blacks in Government National Training Conference, and Coppin State University. Her message always returns to one core belief: **"We all have a story to tell—we just have to be willing to dig deep and find the courage to release it."**

Driven by faith, purpose, and a heart for service, Kimmoly continues to light the way for storytellers ready to impact lives—one book at a time.

www.ingramcontent.com/pod-product-compliance
Lightning Source LLC
Chambersburg PA
CBHW052051270326
41931CB00012B/2716